Am I My Father's Son?

───────

Joe K. Hudson

Am I My Father's Son

Copyright © 2014 by Joe Hudson

All rights reserved. No part of this book may be reproduced or transmitted in any form or by any means without written permission from the author.

ISBN 13: 978-0-9882037-3-0

ISBN: 0988203731

Contents

Introduction	....	ii
Chapter 1	A Change of Direction	1
Chapter 2	Growing Up	9
Chapter 3	Becoming an Adult	22
Chapter 4	Taking Responsibility	28
Chapter 5	A Future With No Hope	40
Chapter 6	A Spiritual Foster Child	56
Chapter 7	Putting the Pieces Together	68
Chapter 8	Weighing the Evidence	84
Chapter 9	Lessons Learned	96

Introduction

This book is an account of how I overcame some of the most difficult challenges I faced during my lifetime.

It is not written to condemn individuals for the unintended consequences of their interactions with me.

It is written to be an encouragement to others. Its purpose is to help them spend their time looking for a solution to their problems rather than focusing entirely on the problem itself.

My sincere desire is that the investment my friends have made in me will provide help to those reading this book.

A Change of Direction

This day dawned as most October days do in the Ozark Mountains. The slight chill in the air was an indication summer had ended and cold weather was just around the corner. The leaves were beginning to turn bright orange, and a few were drifting lazily down from the trees and bouncing softly on the ground below.

For Eddine, a sixteen-year-old mother of two—my mother—it was a sad time of year. She loved the fall colors and the cool weather, but she still had difficulty dealing with memories of an October day just eleven years earlier.

The date was October 28, 1946; eleven years ago today blood poisoning had taken the life of her twenty-six year old mother, Victoria. The blood poisoning resulted from an untreated wound she suffered while working on the family farm. (There was no medication during that time that could prevent this illness. Pennicillin had not yet been discovered.)

Eddine, her sister, and and her two brothers were left behind to fend for themselves. They felt abandoned and they knew they would face tough times for the rest of their lives.

Eddine had given birth to her second son seven days earlier and was still in bed. (In 1946, several days of bed rest was recommended after giving birth.)   Instead of hospital care

A Change of Direction

Eddine was at the home of her husband's parents and was under the care of her mother-in-law and a traveling doctor.

Eddine wondered about the future of both her sons. Maybe they would grow up to become doctors, or maybe one of them would even be president. She realized she had much to be thankful for and she hoped her children would always have the love and encouragement she had needed so desperately after her mother died.

She knew, all too well, the death of her mother had been a life-changing event for her. Before October 28, 1935, exactly eleven years ago today, she was as happy and content as any five year old girl could be. She was enjoying all the happiness her heart could hold from simply crawling up in her mother's lap and knowing she was loved unconditionally. How easy it is to take simple things for granted, she thought.

When her mother died, it was as if someone, or some thing, had forcibly taken her from her happy life and placed her in unfamiliar surroundings. She found herself on a path she had not wanted to take and her life of happiness was nowhere to be found.

For the last eleven years, Eddine's life had been one battle after another. It had taken all her strength just to hang on. She was not in control of her situation and she was certain she would never again be in the driver's seat in her own life. She knew it was childish to cry, but she felt tears of longing rise up in her eyes. She wanted her mother. She desperately needed someone to tell her everything would be OK soon.

Eddine was only five years old when her mother died. No matter how diligently she searched, she had not been able to find a way to fill the void caused by Victoria's death. She knew her dad had tried to help by moving them in with his parents for a short time. She loved her grandmother, but she missed her mother so very much. Eddine always felt she was the most important person in the world to her mother and her mother was always kind even when she was busy.

Nobody could make the awful feeling of helplessness go away or help her deal with the terrible loneliness that had become her constant companion. She remembered crying many long nights until she could cry no more, and finally, in exhaustion, she would drift off into a troubled sleep.

When Eddine's dad married again, her situation went from bad to worse. Now there was a total stranger occupying the place her mother once filled. Eddine didn't like seeing her dad treat a stranger the way he had treated her mother. At the same time, she felt she had also lost her father: this stranger had become more important to him than his children, she thought. Now she would have to deal with a double portion of loneliness as well as an overwhelming feeling of rejection.

A Change of Direction

The new stepmother came burdened with her own troubled past. She also had lost her mother at an early age and had been forced to care for her two brothers and two sisters. It had been very difficult for Eddine to understand why her stepmother would leave a situation where she was raising her own siblings and enter a marriage that required her to care for and raise another group of children that were not her own. These children were not even related to her, but she would be expected to treat them as though they were her own offspring. (Maybe she too was trying to escape the awful feeling of loneliness that comes from losing one's mother.)

While she was living with her father and step-mother Eddine had always felt her stepmother would have preferred to have a house without stepchildren. She had always felt so out-of-place and unwanted She had longed for the times when she was a very important part of the family instead of a step-child. She remembered the times she had felt so secure in her mother's arms and knew her mother loved her more than life itself. Now she found herself doubting that anyone really loved her.

The situation with her stepmother had grown more and more difficult, until finally Eddine felt she could bear the heartache no longer. She made a hasty decision to leave her father's home and start a home of her own. She married at the age of fourteen.

By the time she realized she had made a terrible mistake it was too late to reverse course. She was locked into a lifetime of heartache and misery because the religious beliefs of both her dad and her husband's dad did not allow divorce. She knew if she were to divorce her husband, both sides of her children's family would look upon her as a very bad person. She wanted to be a mother who would make her sons proud, not someone they would have to make excuses for. So she had concluded that divorce would never be an option. She knew she would never be able to make this marriage fulfill her dream of having a home where she would feel loved. She also knew she had no real alternative but to try to make the best of a very bad situation.

While other girls her age were going to school, Eddine was taking care of two children and trying to make a jealous husband happy. She was also working very hard on the small farm to make sure everyone was fed and clothed properly. She now realized that living with her dad and stepmother, as bad as it had been, would have been better than getting married at such an early age.

Even though she loved her sons very much, she couldn't help wishing she had waited a few more years before starting a family of her own.

She had tried with every ounce of her strength to turn a bad marriage into one that was at least bearable. She had prayed

A Change of Direction

for things to be different but by the time her first son was born she knew her situation was never going to improve.

She knew she didn't have time for self-pity so she turned her thoughts back to her current situation. She would have to be strong enough to forget her own happiness and make sure her sons didn't have to face the terrible loneliness and heartache she had suffered. She was determined to do everything within her power to give her sons the best life possible. She would sacrifice her own happiness in an effort to make sure they both knew they were loved.

Just as Eddine had regained her resolve to be strong, her younger sister burst into the room. She was crying and she had a look of sheer terror on her face. After a few minutes Eddine was able to calm her sister down enough to learn what had happened to frighten her.

Her sister had narrowly escaped from my father who had attempted to assault her.

As soon as Eddine managed to get the details from her sister, the would-be attacker crashed through the door and burst into the bedroom. Eddine knew the combined strength of her and her sister would never be enough to defeat the man, so she did the only thing she could do. She blurted out, "I'm going to tell my dad what you did, and he will make you pay dearly for it."

The man, my father, pointed the shotgun he was carrying at my mother's back and pulled the trigger. The shot was fired at such close range that the full load of shotgun pellets ripped through my mother's chest. She died thirty minutes later, leaving behind her two sons. Her resolve to give her children a better life became soneone else's responsibility. She went home to be with her mother.

My mother will never again doubt if she is loved. She traded the rough seas and cold winds of this life for the "still waters" the Bible mentions in Psalm 23 and the warm breezes of heaven, where peace, love, and happiness are the norm instead of the exception.

My father,the man who fired the shot that ended my mother's life, ran away from his father's house and hid in our house a few miles from the scene of the crime.

When law enforcement officers found him, he was huddled inside the house crying like a baby. He sobbed and begged them not to hurt him. He was later declared mentally ill by the court and was placed in a mental institution for several years.

Eddine's two sons, my brother and I, were carried away and placed in the home my mother had attempted to escape from just two years and forty-two days earlier. The same

A Change of Direction

difficulties our mother had faced would now become our challenges.

Sometimes I think my brother was the only really lucky member of our family. He died of unknown causes just fifty days after my mother passed away. The Bible says, "Blessed are the pure in heart because they shall see God." (Mathew 5:8) At fifty days old, I am sure my brother certainly met these requirements. He, my mother, and my grandmother are all in heaven. For that I am grateful.

I was left to make the best of a bad situation, to carry the family torch, and to make whatever impact on this world that would be made by my branch of the Hudson family.

Growing Up

Gaining responsibility for feeding and caring for two more children might have been a more pleasant experience for my step-grandmother if the stork, instead of my grandfather's sister-in-law, had brought my brother and me to her house.

We were not related to her and she only had a few seconds' notice, instead of the normal nine months' gestation period to prepare for new arrivals. It is not difficult to imagine she would be somewhat less than excited about the prospect of having to care for the two of us for the next fifteen or sixteen years.

By the time Marvin Rogers and I arrived, my grandfather and step-grandmother had three children of their own. Now my step-grandmother was expected to care for three of her own children and five children that were not related to her.

My brother's stay at our new home was a very short one. He died in January 1947. I like to think my mother might have been able to convince God to allow at least one of her sons to escape the loneliness she had experienced. I have often wondered why God didn't take me also and make a clean sweep of it. I have to admit, I have wished several times that he had.

Some of my best memories of my early childhood are of my mother's sister, Kathleen. (She was the victim of the attempted assault the day my mother was shot.) I suppose

Growing Up

Kathleen felt she had something in common with me because we were both foster children. She made my life more bearable during those first few years. I have fond memories of sitting in her lap and running my small hands through her silky hair. Kathleen later left home and also married young. She soon realized her marriage had been a mistake, but she ended it and married again. Her second marriage lasted until she died of cancer several years later.

Apart from the constant void inside me, which my mother's love should have filled, life was relatively calm for the first several years after my mother died. But even in the very best of situations, a foster home can never fill all of the hollow places left in the heart of a child when his or her mother is no longer around.

By the time I was five or six years old, my mother's brothers and sisters had moved out on their own, leaving me as the only foster child in the household. My grandfather and step-grandmother would eventually have six children of their own. Three of them were born over the next seven or eight years after I arrived.

I and my half-aunts and my half-uncle grew up in much the same way as most rural children of that time. We had very little money, and most of what we ate was grown on the small farm my grandfather owned. We learned to make our own toys and entertain ourselves with a Prince Albert tobacco can that was bent into a "U" shape and nailed onto a long stick. With this device we were able to chase a round steel band, taken from a wagon wheel, over many miles of dirt road. Or we could chase an old tire for hours on end. In the spring we made whistles from hickory bark, windmills from old pieces of wood, or pop guns from elder bushes.

We really didn't know we were poor, or if we did, nobody seemed to care. My grandfather kept us busy hoeing corn or gathering and canning vegetables from the garden. We would sometimes pick blackberries from wild vines that grew in the pasture. I always thought we probably gathered more chiggers and seed ticks than berries. I know there was almost always "a whole lotta scratchin' goin' on" after we finally brought the berries back home to can.

I am very grateful to my grandfather and my step-grandmother for the extra effort they made to provide food, clothing, and shelter for me while I was growing up.

Life was not easy for them. I can remember my grandfather leaving before sunup to go to work at the sawmill. For most of his adult life, he worked all day and did not return home until after dark. Since he didn't learn to drive until late in life, he walked or caught a ride to work and back.

My grandfather only had a fourth-grade education, but he knew how to provide for his family. If we needed a building to house chickens or some other farm animal, he could build it. He knew how to cure meat so we could have food for the winter. He knew how to find projects for us to do in the summer to keep us out of trouble.

In my own life I could never have accomplished what he did in his. I could not have raised eleven children, even with my master's degree and the salary I have been able to receive.

My step-grandmother was no different. She could make a little go a long, long way. I can remember the large quilt rack hanging in the kitchen. She would sew scrap pieces of cloth together to make a quilt top and then sew flour sacks together to make the back. She tacked the back on the quilt rack, put cotton on it, and begin the long process of sewing the pieces together.

I have many good memories of growing up with my half-aunts and my half-uncle. I am sure we, like all siblings, had many turf battles and petty arguments, but I don't remember those. Instead, I remember the many long summer hours we enjoyed playing together on the small farm.

I especially remember when my step-grandmother conducted what I called her "spring cleaning." This event would last three days. Each morning my step-grandmother lined us all up and fed each of us a spoon full of Black Draught (a very powerful laxative). This made the expression "messing around" take on a whole new meaning for us. We only had a "two-holer" outhouse, and there were seven of us. One does not need a vivid imagination to get a picture of events about two to three hours after the cleaning material had been ingested.

The outdoor toilet was located several yards away from the house, and each of us had to answer two questions before heading toward it: (1) Can I make it that far? (2) Is it occupied?

Needless to say, it was always a good idea to scout the perimeter of the yard and locate a large bush that could cover most of you while the cleaning business was under way. You never knew for sure when it was going to happen to you, but you knew when the feelings started, you were going to make a mess somewhere, and you always hoped it wouldn't be in your pants.

We felt "relieved" when the first round was finished and our bowel movements went back to normal, but we always knew we could look forward to a replay for the next two days.

Despite the fond memories I have of growing up on the farm, like every other human being on the planet, I faced problems that were difficult to overcome. I knew I was not a member of the family, but I am not sure if my feelings of being unwanted directly resulted from how others acted toward me, or if knowing I belonged to another family colored my perspective. Whichever was the case, I remember lying awake at night crying and wishing I knew for sure someone loved me the way only a mother can.

Growing Up

Sometimes a person's situation may seem normal simply because he or she may not realize that it could be different, but after a few years I began to question some of the things that happened to me.

My uncle, who was four years older than me, usually slept in the same bed with me. Sometimes when I got up in the morning, the bed would be wet because someone had urinated in the night. I never remembered peeing in the bed, and when I spent the night with my cousins, I never wet the bed, so I was not sure what was going on.

One morning my step-grandmother sat me down in a chair in front of the other children and rubbed the piss-soaked sheet in my face. I think she did this in an effort to stop the bed-wetting. I was the child, and she was the adult, so the message I received from this experience was that I was something less than a child who deserved to be loved

After this I began to feel my whippings were coming too often and with little or no justification. One day after I had reached the point where I couldn't take the abuse anymore, my step-grandmother came at me with a "switch" raised and ready to strike. I refused to allow her to whip me, and she backed off. That ended my encounters with the switch. My step-grandmother and I both had reached the conclusion that I had outgrown that kind of punishment.

When I was about eight or nine years old, my grandfather called me aside. He said he wanted to talk to me about something. We took a walk, and he told me that his sister-in-law had told him my father had been released from the mental hospital and that he had told his brother-in-law he was coming to kill us (my grandfather and me).

I remember being scared to death. My fear was made worse by the fact that my bedroom was like a back porch, separated from the rest of the house, and when I turned in for the night, I had to go into this dark room to go to bed alone. I was afraid my father was going to be hiding in the closet with his shotgun and that he would blow my brains out. For an eight year old, or anyone else for that matter, this was a pretty heavy load to carry. I would always turn on the light by pulling the string attached to the light in the center of the room. Then I would look in the closet and under the bed to make sure he was not there.

I was just learning to cope with this threat when another bombshell dropped. My uncle and I were fighting, and my step-grandmother yelled out the door at me and said, "You're going to grow up to be a murderer just like your dad." For a young boy already struggling to feel good about himself, this was a devastating blow. Young children take to heart the words of adults, and this statement haunted me for at least twenty-five years. I was certain my step-grandmother saw something in me that indicated I would grow up to be a murderer.

Growing Up

My misunderstanding of the "Christian" religion also became a problem for me. My grandfather always took us to a church where the preachers, as I remember, were mostly "hellfire and damnation" preachers. One of the sermons I heard has stayed with me all these years. The preacher, whose name I can't remember, said there was a sin God would not forgive. He failed to say what the sin was. He said if you did this thing, you could never be saved, and God would burn you forever. He also said there would never be an end to the awful burning pain.

I had burned my hand on the wood stove we used to heat the house, so I knew from experience how it felt to be burned. This was the worst pain I had ever experienced, and I could imagine God burning me so that I would feel this awful pain all over my body, a pain I would feel forever with no hope for relief.

After all this, now when I went to bed I had to deal with the loneliness, the fear that the man who had killed my mother was going to blow my brains out, the concern that I might grow up to be a murderer, and the anxiety that I might accidentally commit the unpardonable sin and God would roast me over an open flame forever.

I began to develop an intense hatred for the man who killed my mother and ruined my life. I became very bitter, and I started blaming him for everything that had gone wrong in my life. I promised myself that this man was going to pay for all the pain and suffering he had caused and that I was going to be the person who made it happen.

Unfortunately for me, my focus was almost entirely on my problems. I began to see everything through the prism of my troubles. This led me to believe, rightly or wrongly, that I was someone who was undeserving of anyone's love.

One afternoon after school, an older student from the high school stopped by my elementary school. While we were all waiting outside the school building for the school bus to pick us up and take us home, he started poking fun at me and slapping me around in front of my girlfriend and my classmates. I can still remember my girlfriend standing there watching him, and I couldn't understand why she would still care about me because the older student was making me cry. Why she would care about a crybaby was more than I could understand.

Finally the principal came by, and I asked him to make the older boy stop. The principal just nonchalantly took the hand of a young second grader, started walking away, and said to me, "There's nothing I can do for you." If the principal had just turned to the older boy and said one word, "Quit," my situation would have been greatly improved. I don't know why the principal was unwilling to help me. Maybe he was too afraid of the older student to say anything, or maybe he thought any effort at this time would do little or nothing to improve my overall situation.

Growing Up

I saw the principal several years later, and he asked how I was doing. I naturally gave him a glowing report of my current situation. He said, "You were dumped into the sewer, but it looks like you came out smelling like a rose." I strongly suspected he remembered the day I asked him for a small amount of help and he walked away, leaving me in my misery.

Even practical jokes, which were common in the culture in which I grew up, became attacks to me. Once my cousin and I were clearing rocks out of a bicycle trail when a scorpion stung me. Some of the adults that were there with us told me the scorpion was poisonous and that it would kill me. This was meant as a practical joke, but I really believed I was dying, and I couldn't understand why I was worth so little that no one seemed to care at all. Looking back, I am certain they didn't understand that what they had done had just reinforced my low opinion of myself.

By the time I was a junior in high school, my situation had become even more difficult for me. By then, since I had never been told what it was, I had decided the unforgiveable sin must be thinking or saying something against God. The battle that raged in my mind was intense and never-ending.

I finally developed a method to prevent myself from thinking something that would offend God and give him cause to banish me to hell. Because I had concluded that God didn't really want us to think highly of ourselves, every time I had a positive thought I would start trying to think negative thoughts about myself instead. I don't remember how I came up with this idea, but I suppose I needed an answer, and this was the only one I could find.

Needless to say, it doesn't take long for this practice to make one's self-esteem plummet. Several studies have proved that it takes as many as five to sixteen positive statements to overcome one negative comment, and the math was not in my favor. I was losing ground fast.

Since I had developed such a low opinion of myself, I naturally assumed everyone else saw me the same way I saw myself. This made it impossible for me to find someone to fill the void in my life. It also became impossible for me to believe anyone could ever really care about me.

It is amazing to me that, no matter how difficult life becomes, there always seems to be something, real or imagined, to hang on to drifting nearby. During this low point in my life, I fell head over heels in love with one of the girls in my school. I would lie awake at night and pretend to hold her close to me, but I knew, or thought I knew, she would never feel the same way about me. She was my dream girl, but unfortunately she was mine *only* in my dreams.

I never told her the way I felt about her because I was never sure the feeling was mutual, and I did not want to be rejected by her. To me she was perfect in every way, and I knew

Growing Up

even my dreams would be shattered if she didn't feel the same way about me.

For a few fleeting moments, my imagined relationship gave me an escape from my self-pity and my poor self-image. For this I am grateful.

About halfway through my junior year in high school, I had finally arrived at the point where I just didn't care much about anything anymore. Looking back, I think this was probably the lowest point in my life.

I made the decision to drop out of high school, but, fortunately for me, some of my classmates had different plans for my life. One day I left my books behind and headed toward the door of the school building, ready to leave for good. I was about to increase the speed of my downward spiral; I had no idea what lay ahead.

But as I was about to exit the building, several classmates, including Rosemary Breedlove (my aunt) and Delberta House, caught up with me and convinced me to stay in school. I don't recall the words they spoke, but I do recall the sincerity with which they said them. I was drowning. As a matter of fact I was going under the third time and they threw me a lifeline.

I finished high school because these classmates cared. I finished college because they cared. Probably everything good that happened to me after this is a direct result of their actions on that day. I owe them a debt of gratitude that is far above my ability to repay.

A few years ago I told my aunt, Rosemary, her comments that day had a significant impact on my life. I also told Delberta, but I have not shared this story with the other classmates who were there with them. Nor have I shared with Delberta and Rosemary the real story behind my decision to drop out of school.

The English language, at least my vocabulary, does not contain words that adequately describe the amount of help these people gave me. I am deeply indebted to them for their very wise words and their genuine concern for my future.

For most of the members of our class, graduation meant leaving school and entering the workforce. This made the two-week trip called the "senior trip", taken at the end of the last semester, a welcome vacation. I have fond memories of visiting Elvis Presley's mansion, the Grand Ole Opry, and the beach at Pensacola, Florida.

After returning from this trip it was time for me to trade my books for a paper hat worn by employees at the chicken processing plant where I would spend the next several months learning another one of life's many important lessons.

Becoming an Adult

My first job after graduating high school was running a "lung gun" at a chicken processing plant in Springdale, Arkansas. This job made me realize that additional education was an absolute necessity unless I wanted to spend the rest of my life watching chicken butts go by on an assembly line.

Since my father was a disabled veteran, I was entitled to funds for higher education from the Veterans Administration. Their required aptitude test indicated that a computer related field was a good fit for me, so I enrolled in a vocational technical school in Morrilton, Arkansas and later received a diploma in electronic data processing.

My choice of careers has proven to be the correct one. But, halfway through the education program I made a snap decision to get married. Unfortunately for my new bride and myself, I brought my troubles along as a dowry.

My wife was only seventeen years old and I was barely twenty. Neither of us were mature enough for the responsibilities of married life and each of us came with unrealistic expectations for the marriage.

Neither of us met the expectations of the other, so for the first several years, we spent a significant amount of money on attorney fees as we both tried to file for divorce on multiple occasions.

Our first child was born after thirteen months. It was a little girl, and I thought then—as I still do—that she was the most beautiful person I had ever seen. Even though we now had an additional member of the family, our family's situation had not improved at all. The cold war between my wife and I raged on.

Politicians had not yet declared the use of birth control pills a sin in the 1960's. (I suppose we had real issues back then.) So, in order to prevent pregnancy, my wife took these. Somehow she still became pregnant, and another child—my son—was born into the family on October 21, 1969. This was the same month and day my brother had been born twenty-three years earlier. My son always thought there was some special meaning to this.

Sadly, the arrival of our second child did nothing to reduce the fighting between my wife and myself.

I wasn't sure if divorce was the sin God would not forgive, but I had been taught it was a very bad thing. Even though I knew several church-going persons who had divorced and remarried, I was not excited about taking the chance of committing the unknown, unforgiveable sin.

(I later learned that all commandments and regulations of biblical law have an equal footing. James 2:10 says, "For whosoever shall keep the whole law, and yet offend in one point, he is guilty of all." In other words, being disobedient to God is sin no matter which law one breaks. Therefore, breaking any particular law is not something God will not forgive.)

I had misunderstood a Bible verse in the book of Matthew, "Whosoever putteth away his wife…causes her to commit adultery" (Matt 5:32, KJV). I thought it meant if we divorced, I would be responsible for my former wife committing adultery.

The New International Version translation of Matthew 5:32 gives a clearer meaning of the verse: "But I tell you that anyone who divorces his wife…makes her the victim of adultery." The verse does not mean that one person is responsible for another person's sins. Even if I had tried, I could not have been responsible for any sin my wife might commit. Basically, to put away one's wife without a biblical reason and then marry someone else is to commit adultery. Divorcing a wife without a biblical cause is a start in this direction, so the verse simply means a man has wronged his spouse by divorcing her, not that he causes the spouse to sin when she remarries.

I was also reluctant to get a divorce because I did not like the idea of my children calling someone else "Daddy." Nor did I want someone else teaching my kids right and wrong.

The continuous fighting only lowered my self-esteem, and our relationship went from bad to worse. I think the worst part of a bad marriage is never being certain how many of the problems are one's own fault and how many are the other person's fault. I know I prayed long and hard for God to fix my marriage, but it seemed to me He was not in the marriage-fixing business at the time.

I remembered a statement made by a church member who was a divorcee. He said, "God will answer most any prayer except those dealing with a bad marriage." I couldn't help but believe he might be right because God sure didn't seem to be interested in answering my prayer.

I later apologized to my daughter for bringing her up in such a battle zone. Her comment to me was: "I was angry about this for some time, but I now realize marriage is a difficult undertaking in the best of circumstances." She had been married for several years when she said this.

Looking back, I am not sure how many of our marital problems were a direct result of my troubled past. Nor am I sure divorce would not have been the best approach to solving our marital problems. Our constant fighting and mutual disrespect certainly did nothing to ensure a happy life. I *am* sure, however, that healing only comes to a marriage when each individual accepts responsibility for his or her own actions and respects the feelings of his or her spouse. Marriage is a partnership and should be treated as such. If ever there is a place to apply the golden rule ("Treat others as you would be treated"), marriage is certainly the place. This rule is hard to apply when one or both individuals are angry with the other.

      I suspect there is always more than enough blame to go around so that both parties make a significant contribution to the failure, or success, of any endeavor. I also suspect that the failure of either individual to recognize and correct his or her own mistakes is a guaranteed formula for failure.

Am I My Father's Son?

Taking Responsibility

Before I learned that many of my problems were really caused by my own actions, I was just sinking deeper into the mire of self-pity. As long as I believed that some one, or some thing, other than myself was responsible for my failures, I was a slave to whatever I believed was causing the problem.

It is true that the action of others had caused great difficulty in my life. But, it is also true that I allowed the hurt to continue well beyond the point it should have gone. My life was not under the control of others. I could choose how to handle whatever life had thrown at me and I could throw off the bondage through my own actions.

The following story by an unknown author puts my situation into perspective.

> A little bird waited too long to fly south for the winter. By the time he started on its journey, the weather had gotten so cold that the bird froze up and fell to the ground in a large field. While he was lying there, a cow came by and dropped dung on him. As the frozen bird lay there in the pile of cow dung, he began to realize how warm it was. The dung was actually thawing him out! He lay there all warm and happy, and soon began to sing for joy. A passing cat heard the bird singing and came to investigate. Following the

sound, the cat discovered the bird under the pile of cow dung and promptly dug him out and ate him!

The morals of this story are:

- Not everyone who drops manure on you is your enemy.
- Not everyone who gets you out of manure is your friend.
- And when you're in deep dung, keep your mouth shut!

Even though I had reached the conclusion I could never dig my way out of the hole I found myself in, help was already on its way.

One night I had a dream that taught me a very valuable lesson. The lesson was that success in life does not come because we are problem-free. Rather, success comes when we convert the negative energy of anger, worry, and self-pity; energy that is produced by our problems, into the extra positive energy we need to accomplish our goals.

In my dream I had a large rope draped over my shoulder, and I was struggling very hard to pull something behind me. Eventually the load became so heavy that I couldn't pull it any farther. No matter how hard I pulled on the rope, I was not able to move it at all. Finally, I gave up and sat down on a large rock

Taking Responsibility

at the edge of the path. As far as I was concerned, forward movement was no longer possible for me.

When I sat down, I looked behind me at the burden I was dragging, and, to my astonishment, I saw that the other end of the rope was tied around the yoke, just below the handlebars, of a lightweight English racer–type bicycle. I then climbed on the bicycle and started riding it.

I woke up and gave the dream some very serious thought. It dawned on me I had finally discovered the real problem with my life. It was not that other people had done something to me they should not have done. It was a lack of ability, on my part, to recognize opportunity. I had discovered that I was my own worst enemy. As Walt Kelly said in his cartoon *Pogo*, "We have met the enemy and he is us." My burden was about to become my source of energy.

Now the task that lie head was to put my problems, both real and perceived, behind me. Some problems would take several years to overcome, some would never be solved completely, and some needed my immediate attention.

Each of my problems actually represented a deficiency. They would never solve themselves nor would they ever go away on their own. It would be up to me to decide whether to take positive action or just sit back and dig deeper into the chasm I had already built for myself.

Upward movement held a definite appeal, so I started trying to look inward at my own actions rather than outward to the action of others.

The first step in my recovery was to attack my feeling of negative self-worth. I felt less intelligent than others around me, so now I resolved to make that feeling my partner and friend instead of my enemy; we would combine forces and defeat the real problem, my ignorance. My feelings were actually telling me the truth. I was not as educated as some of the people around me. It had been so much easier to blame others for my ignorance than to accept responsibility for it myself.

It had been almost twenty years since my graduation from high school and I knew it would not be an easy task, but I also knew it would be a good feeling to know that I was on the same level as my associates.

I moved my family to Dallas, Texas, and started my college education at Dallas Baptist College. I later transferred my credits to Southwest Baptist University in Bolivar, Missouri, and graduated with a bachelor's degree in business administration and a minor in religious studies. This was twenty-one years after I had graduated from Jasper High School in Jasper, Arkansas. I

Taking Responsibility

later received a master's degree in political science from Arkansas State University in Jonesboro, Arkansas.

While my feelings of being inferior were certainly very difficult to overcome, the "granddaddy" of all my problems was dealing with the man who killed my mother. After all, I had given him most of the credit for causing me to be in this situation in the first place.

I realized the time had come for me to take control of this problem and wrestle it to the ground. I drove to Harrison, Arkansas, and found the man who, I thought, was responsible for making my life such a wreck.

A great dreal of time, and prayer, had gone into the preperation for this confrontation, but I was determined to put an end to all the heartache this man had caused me.

When I arrived at his house, he was standing on the front porch. I had everything planned down to the last detail, and I didn't waste time. I approached him and when my eyes met his, I said these words: "Dad, I don't know how to tell you this, but I do care for you." He knew those words really meant "I forgive you."

I saw the tears start to stream down his cheeks, and he could not hold back his sobbing. He turned and went back into the house, and I didn't see him again until I buried him a few weeks later. I am so grateful I did this before he died. Moral: Take care of what you know you need to do today. Tomorrow is not promised.

During my seven- or eight-hour drive from Harrison, Arkansas, to Dallas, Texas, I was spilling years of heartache all over the highway. I was letting my pain go, and it would never return to haunt me again. All the hatred I had felt for my father seeped out of me like a leaky faucet. The anxiety caused by years of turning on the light and looking under my bed to make sure he was not going to kill me melted away like snow under the warm sunshine.

I had discovered that even though his actions had caused me a lifetime of heartache, I was the only one that could put limits on the damage they would cause.

My destiny was now in my own hands, and no one else could keep me from it without my permission. I had discovered that forgiving a person is not letting him or her off the hook; it is preventing that person from doing further damage. I had thrown a saddle on this problem, and I was determined to hang on until it was gentle enough to ride.

A few weeks later I received a call saying that my dad had passed away. I hate to think what my life would have become if I had not gotten rid of the hatred I had for him before he died. I

Taking Responsibility

regret not sitting him down and making him tell me his side of the story. It might have made a difference, but I'll never know.

I did learn my dad was "shell-shocked" in World War II. When I was young, I was taught this meant he was a coward, but I have since learned this trauma can happen to even the bravest men.

My fear of growing up to be a "coward like my dad" was not an easy burden to overcome, but I finally learned that all people experience fear. The difference between being a coward and being brave is facing and controlling your fear instead of allowing your fear to control you. I concluded that not many seven- or eight-year-old boys would walk into a dark room believing someone might be hiding there ready to blow their brains out with a shotgun. I knew no coward would face his or her fear this way, but I had faced mine in just this fashion many times. I realized I had never been a coward. I was finally beginning to see the real me, and I was pleased with what I saw.

I still had other problems. One of them was that I still remembered my step-grandmother's words, "You are going to grow up to be a murderer just like your dad." I struggled with these words for years, but I finally reached the following conclusions:

- His blood flows through my veins.
- Half my DNA comes from him.
- I have his big nose.
- I have his black hair.
- I walk like he does.
- Even though I was not around him while I was growing up, my mannerisms are similar to his.

Physically I am my father's son. He is the link in the ancestral chain that makes me a part of the Hudson family. However, my character and my personality are what I choose to make them.

I made a decision that I could be the son of my father without making the same mistakes he had made. I decided the sexual desires I had were given to me by God and were not bad. It didn't mean I would rape someone because I was attracted to her. I also learned that anger is a part of every human being, and if I became angry at someone, it didn't mean I was a murderer. I was compleyely free to fulfill my own destiny.

After I realized all this, I didn't need to worry about doing something bad simply because I was the offspring of someone who had committed a horrible crime. Yes, I am my natural father's son, but I am not exactly like him: I am a good son to my father even though I never believed he was a good father to me. I cannot escape the fact that it is my responsibility to carry on the family torch and carry it to the best of my ability.

Taking Responsibility

When my father died, I buried him in a grave next to my mother and my brother. I knew my mother and brother had forgiven him also, and, for better or worse, we are family.

I talked with my father before he died and asked him if he was a "Christian." He said he was, so I knew God had forgiven him too. "Though your sins be as scarlet, they shall be as white as snow" (Isa 1:18).

My dad drew a monthly pension from the Veterans Administration, and he had saved part of it. I gave about 10 percent of his savings to a small church to pay off an outstanding bank loan. I didn't tell the church members why I gave them the money, but I asked God to accept this on behalf of my father because I knew my father did not give much, if anything, to the church.

The valuable lesson I had learned was that by accepting responsibility for my own actions I could learn to love myself and become the person I wanted to be. I could also use my problems and my low self-esteem as fuel to propel me beyond where I might have gone without them.

I missed my mother then, and I still miss her now. In my mind she is second only to Eve in perfection. God created Eve with his own hands. I believe God created the reproductive process, and all humans since Adam and Eve have been made through it. However, mankind can interfere with this, and therefore, no human being is as perfect as the ones God made with his own hands.

Although I've learned to use my problems to my benefit, still, if I had a choice, I would trade the life I have lived without a mother for a life with her. I can only imagine what it would be like to have her near to dry my tears, patch my skinned knees, and offer me the encouragement and love only a mother can give.

In summary, because of my dad's actions, I was placed where I didn't choose to go, was kept there longer than I wanted to stay, and endured heartaches I didn't want to endure. But I was not defeated. I was actually made stronger by the experience.

And I would like to say to you, Mom, you did help me find the life you wanted for me. Even in death you pointed the way. I learned you were in heaven a few years after you died when I stood by your gravestone and read this inscription:

> Whose departure was grievous to our hearts, but not without hope.
>
> Trusting by her own evidence that she was prepared to go.

Taking Responsibility

As I read the poem etched in the limestone of your grave marker, I was also reminded that someday I too would be required to exchange this life for one that lasts forever:

> Remember friends as you pass by.
> As you are now, so once was I.
> As I am now, so you must be.
> So prepare for death, and follow me.

You helped encourage me to follow in your footsteps. Thank you.

When I stood over your grave, I made a pledge to become a living monument to you. When I meet you again, I trust you will know that I gave my best effort to keep the pledge.

I sincerely hope you will be as proud to call me your son as I am to call you my mother.

Am I My Father's Son?

A Future with No Hope

Even though learning to make the most of my time on this earth had been a very challenging struggle, dealing with the possibility of my eternal existence was even more difficult.

Since the Christian religion was the only religion I knew, I turned to the Bible for answers about eternity. However, I found the Bible to be a book that is very easily misunderstand. Instead of finding peace and joy in the promise of a utopian after-death experience, I found a fear of rejection and pain, both for this life and for the afterlife.

Many church pastors agree that a difficult experience with family life all but guarantees a difficult experience with spiritual life. This was certainly true for me.

The Bible refers to God as our spiritual father, but the word "father" meant someone who took my mother's life and created circumstances that would lead to my brother's death. This made it extremely difficult for me to see God as someone who would love and protect me.

The mental picture of God I had painted from sermons I heard during most of my youth was not one of someone who loved me, or even liked me. I had concluded that He was more in the business of punishing people than in the business of loving and protecting them. I drew a parallel between what my father had done to me, and what God would do to me if I couldn't measure up to his standards.

My first personal experience with religion came shortly after I graduated from high school. One of the preachers came to our house for Sunday dinner. He wanted to pray with me, so I said that would be OK. After he finished, he thought I had been saved, but I didn't. He insisted, so I went to church a few times after this, but I still didn't think I had been saved.

I was told a person's salvation wasn't completed until he or she made a public declaration of it, so I stood up in church one night and told the congregation I had been saved. This didn't seem to help my situation either. After that, I only attended church a few more times.

I was uncertain about my status as a Christain and I found an excuse to bail out when, during a Sunday morning church service, an argument erupted between the preacher and another church member. It would be several years before I would return to church after this.

The procedure for obtaining salvation at the church we attended was an obstacle for me also. When the preacher finished his sermon, the congregation would sing a song, and the preacher would invite people who wanted to be saved to come to the front of the church and kneel at a long bench that was used for an altar. The individual seeking salvation would cry and, it seemed to me, beg God to save him or her. I was never sure I could do that. Or at least, I was absolutely certain that if I did, I wouldn't be able to do it correctly.

One day I became afraid that I would not be allowed to go to heaven, so I promised God if he would cause the preacher to preach on healing, I would know that I could be saved and that I would become a Christian.

I took my family to church the next time it gathered, and the preacher did preach on healing. This was a church, and a pastor, that had never practiced, or preached, healing. Because of this I knew God had answered my prayer, but I was afraid I couldn't cry and beg the way I thought I was expected to do. Instead of going up to the front of the church, I just thought in my mind that if I believed in Christ, I would be saved. I told God I believed that Jesus was the Son of God.

Several years went by, and I didn't make any effort to attend church. Then, during one of the times my wife and I were separated, I was baptized and became a member of a Baptist church. Looking back, I am not sure I did this for any other reason than to try to save my marriage. Since I had little real commitment to religion, in very short order I dropped out of church and turned my attention to other things.

One evening I came home late and picked up the Bible. It fell opened to the tenth chapter of Hebrews, and I started reading from there. I read through the twenty-sixth verse: "For if we sin willfully after having received the knowledge of the truth, there remaineth no more sacrifice for sins." On the surface this verse seems to say if God has forgiven us of our sins and we commit another sin, we are lost again and can never be saved. In other words, it seems to say we are just waiting to die so we can spend a long forever in hell.

I had no idea what this verse really meant, but what it meant to me was that I had started out going to church and quit. Therefore, my destiny had been sealed. I was going to burn for a very long eternity. The only thing I could look forward to was being roasted over an open flame for eternity. Needless to say, this did not fill me with great joy and gladness.

Several days later I timidly tried to read the Bible again, thinking I might find something I had missed. This time I read about Esau in Hebrews 12:17: "For ye know how that afterward, when he would have inherited the blessing, he was rejected: for he found no place of repentance, though he sought it carefully with tears."

All the memories of the sermon about the unpardonable sin I had heard as a youth came flooding back. I couldn't believe I had fought so hard for so many years to avoid this sin, and now maybe this was it. It didn't seem fair to me that a person could

A Future With no Hope

simply find himself or herself locked out of heaven without any hope whatsoever.

    For the next several years I spent a lot of time worrying about what I thought was my new status: being lost without hope. Then one night I had a dream in which my great-grandmother, who had been a devout Christian, appeared to me. She said to me, "God has sent me to tell you that you have stepped into God." I didn't know what "stepped into God" meant, but I was certain it was not good. I remember the feeling of hopelessness I experienced when she made that statement. Like a person drowning, I reached up and grabbed her hand, hoping for help, and then I woke up. I will never forget how her hand felt in mine. It was pliable and soft. When I grasped it, it bent as though it were some sort of soft plastic.

    I started to attend church again, hoping I might do something to get God to change his mind and not send me to hell. I guess I was trying to force myself on him. Religion had become exactly what the rest of my life had been. I was attending church services, but I did not feel like I was "one of the family." And I was even more convinced I was not someone God would want in his group of chosen people.

    On July 4, 1977, I visited with a pastor of a small church, and I suppose he sensed some of my struggles. He asked me the following question: "Do you think God would lie?" It was a trap I couldn't avoid. I didn't believe God would lie, but even if I did, I was too frightened of him to say so aloud. The pastor went on to quote Romans 10:9: "That if thou shalt confess with thy mouth the Lord Jesus, and shalt believe in thine heart that God hath raised him from the dead, thou shalt be saved." Then he quoted Romans 10:13: "For whosoever shall call upon the name of the Lord shall be saved."

The pastor told me I was "saved," and I needed to be baptized. I was baptized again and became a member of this church. But my nagging doubts about my relationship with God and whether he had really accepted me still lingered. I was told God expected his people to give a tithe of ten percent of their income. I didn't think God would want this tithe from me, so I had my wife give it instead, in the hope that maybe he would accept it from her on my behalf.

In the Southern Baptist Church, each local church observes two ordinances: baptism and the Lord's Supper. A person must undergo the first one, baptism, to become a member of the church. The second one, the "Lord's Supper," was observed periodically. When the church observed the "Lord's Supper," the preacher would always quote 1 Corinthians 11:27 before starting this service: "Wherefore whosoever shall eat this bread, and drink this cup of the Lord, unworthily, shall be guilty of the body and blood of the Lord."

A Future With no Hope

I didn't feel accepted by God, and I was afraid he would kill me if I took part in the service, so when my turn came, I refused to participate. I later learned what the verse really meant. It refers more to the manner in which the ordinance is conducted than to the persons participating. I am still not sure why the meaning was not explained in the service at that time. I discovered later that some pastors simply do what everyone else does with little or no effort to find the true meaning of scripture.

Since I didn't seem to be getting any closer to my goal of getting God to accept me, I felt it was time for a new approach. I thought maybe there was something more I needed to do so, I became a preacher. The local church ordained me, and I became a bivocational (part-time) pastor. Instead of causing me to reside on "easy street," this decision created a new set of challenges.

One Sunday morning while I was serving as pastor of a small church in Arkansas a former pastor attended the service. He also brought with him a seminary professor. I had just barely made it through high school, and the only Bible instruction I had received was the sermons I heard while I was growing up. I felt very inadequate. Who was I to be teaching these two about the Bible when they knew much more about it than I did?

My situation reminded me of a joke I had heard earlier, which goes something like this:

One of the survivors of the Jonestown flood finally died and went to heaven. St. Peter met him at heaven's gate and asked if there was anything he could do for him to make his stay more pleasant. The gentleman said, "Yes. I'm sure you know how much I like to tell the story of the Jonestown flood. I would like an audience so I can tell them all about it." St. Peter gathered an audience and started introducing the speaker. During the introduction St. Paul leaned over and whispered in the speaker's ear, "I guess you probably know Noah is sitting in the audience."

Religion was not the only area in which I felt I lacked knowledge. I had worked with computers for several years with little or no formal education in computer science. I felt less capable than some of the people I worked with, so I knew I needed to get a better education in this field also.

I moved the family to Dallas, Texas, with the intention of completing a bachelor of arts degree at Dallas Baptist University and then a doctorate at the Baptist Theological Seminary in Fort Worth.

After completing thirty hours at Dallas Baptist University, I learned I could complete course work at other colleges and transfer them back to Dallas Baptist anf still graduate from Dallas Baptist. With that in mind, I moved the family back to Arkansas and completed two semesters at the University of Central Arkansas.

Instead of transferring my credit hours back to Dallas Baptist, I decided to transfer my courses from both colleges to Southwest Baptist University in Bolivar, Missouri. I completed my undergraduate degree there.

When I started my course work at Southwest Baptist, I was also pastoring a small church in Arkansas. During this time, my wife and I separated again. Based on 1 Timothy 3, I felt if God had wanted me to be a church pastor, he would have given me the ability to keep my marriage together. I changed my major to business administration and graduated with a B.A. in this field.

I finally gave up pastoring and decided to try a different profession. Even though I believed in the Bible and all it taught, I didn't believe in myself. I could never really believe that God believed in me either. Nor did I believe he really wanted me in heaven. I just could not continue to sell something to others that I was not convinced applied to me.

Somehow I was under the impression it was a preacher's responsibility to do something that would save others. Later I realized that God is the one who does the saving, and preachers just introduce individuals to him. I also learned the responsibility of individual Christians was not to save people either. Their role is simply to plant the seed and let God do the work of conversion.

I was caught up in the traditional religious practice of "hitting people over the head with the Bible" in an attempt to change their behavior. It didn't work on me, and I was not convinced it would work for others either.

After ending my attempts at pastoring churches, I decided to try my hand at politics. There was a big push by religious leaders at that time for Christians to participate in the political system, and I thought this might be a way I could make a difference in the lives of others.

It wasn't long until I learned that several of those politicians who were beating the "Christian" drums the loudest were not even close to being Christlike. As a mater of fact, I found that those who seek office on the "I'm a Christian" platform, were the absolute worst candidates for public office. They do more damage to government and to "Christianity" than all the others combined.

They pretend to be very concerned about the unborn.. The reality is their actions indicate they are more concerned about keeping the abortion issue alive than they are in resolving it. This allows them to use the same emotional issue to deceive their followers again the next election cycle.

A Future With no Hope

During my time as a state representative, a piece of legislation that would ban partial-birth abortion was taken up by the Arkansas Legislature.

The way this bill was handled by these people made it abundantly clear to me that their primary objective was to pretend to do one thing while they were actually accomplishing something else.

The bill passed the House with an overwhelming majority, and when the Senate considered it, the Senate members placed an amendment in it to protect the life and health of the mother. These so-called representatives of the Christian faith opposed this amendment even though they knew the US Supreme Court would never allow the law to be enforced without it.

These same legislators did not honor Christ with their campaign practices either. They were running false political ads against their opponents and they knew these ads were lies. They did not honor Christ, nor did they emulate him. The Jesus I know would never have to resort to sin in order to accomplish his righteous purpose. Those that did not accept Christianity as the way to heaven just simply pointed to the actions of these people and said, "See. I told you there is nothing to Christianity."

Most of us know that some political candidates stretch the truth frequently, but I couldn't find anywhere in the Bible that Christians were given the right to lie and cheat when they were seeking political office. Christians are to be Christlike in everything they do. "In **all** thy ways acknowledge him and he will derect thy path." (Proverbs 3:6)

My biggest disappointment was that some churches were on the "bandwagon" and supported this kind of behavior. They invited some of these politicians to speak from their pulpits as though they were messengers from God.

I believed strongly that the hypocritical actions of these politicians were not advancing the kingdom of God, and I wanted no part of them. The Bible says the kingdom of Christ is not of this world.(John 18:36) It also says that Satan is the god of this world.(II Cor 4:4) In my opinion, their actions were advancing the kingdom of the god of this world.

It is difficult to understand how these people are so successful at deceiving so many people, especially those who may have thought they were actually doing a service for God.

Unfortunately, I was operating under the false assumption that people make rational decisions based on facts. I finally discovered the majority of voters do not make their own decisions; they depend on others to do their thinking for them. This allows strong-willed individuals to lead the average voter around by the neck and get him or her to do whatever they ask. Such individuals can misquote scripture and lead the masses like sheep to the slaughter.

It became obvious to me that a large number of people who claim to be Christian have no idea what the Bible really says about the hot political issues of our time. The overwhelming majority of these people never study the Bible, and since politicians have now taken over the task of explaining what the Bible means, these unlearned "Christians" have simply become political pawns.

After my disappointing experience with politics, I started looking for another way to make a difference in people's lives. In an effort to help individuals think for themselves, I started teaching U.S. government and Texas government in a Dallas County, Texas, community college. I wanted to encourage individuals to stop being so cognitively lazy and to learn to make their own decisions based on facts. I did this for seven years, and felt I did help a few students.

In an effort to get my students to find truth about political issues, I gave them assignments that forced them to research the history of each issue. Many were surprised to find information that contradicted the sound bites that have become such an integral part of our political process. Some were also surprised to learn their own pastors were so careless with the truth about these issues.

But still, after learning, preaching, teaching, and governing, I was still no closer to finding the answers about God that I needed. I didn't know it at this time, but I was to find out later that God had me right where he wanted me.

Confusion reigned supreme in my attempt to be a Christian. I had discovered that what others were saying and doing did not agree with my idea of truth. I had previously accepted statements made by church members and pastors, but now these statements didn't seem to work for me because I realized they were based on emotion, not biblical fact. One person had said, "If you don't know you're saved, you're not saved." This seemed to indicate if you had a bad day and you were lacking in faith, you had never been saved in the first place.

Another said if you don't remember the time and the date of your conversion, you are not saved. I wasn't sure what happened to those who had suffered memory loss.

I found that too many churchgoers have a religious experience and assume everyone else is supposed to have the exact same experience. I later learned that not everyone reacts the same way to anything, not even religion.

When I wanted to know the truth about my earthly father's intention to take my life, I put myself in a situation where

A Future With no Hope

he had an opportunity to do so if that was what he wanted. He didn't, so I knew my fear of him was unfounded. But how do you test God to see if he really wants to banish you into the flames of hell? As far as I knew, there was no way for us to stick our heads through a window into heaven and to see what he would do with each of us—no trial run is available. I know of no acquaintance of mine who has died and then come back because he or she didn't like what was on the other side.

According to the Bible, there are those who go through life doing what they believe is right, only to wind up losing their chance of entering heaven: "Not everyone that saith unto me, Lord, Lord shall enter into the kingdom of heaven; but he that doeth the will of my father which is in heaven." (Matt 7:21). This verse seems to indicate that some people will go through life thinking they are on their way to heaven but actually will be in for a big surprise when they die and go the other direction.

Since I didn't want to tell anyone I thought God was planning to burn me forever, I knew of no person on earth I could talk to about my problems or turn to for help.

If we think our situation is unique to us and no other person on earth has had, or will have, the same experience, then we assume there is no way out. It is a catch-22: as long as we believe there is no hope of finding a solution to our problem, we will never be aggressive in searching for it. We can actually box ourselves into a situation that seems to have no escape.

Hope is the fuel we need to propel us forward until the next goal is reached. At this point in my life my "hope tank" had gone past empty; I was running on fumes. Needless to say, my expectation for the future was something far less than hopeful.

A Spiritual Foster Child

Based on some of my experiences in life I had concluded that I was bad—not a person who had done bad things, but a bad person in my very essence. Even though I could not identify anything I had done to cause this condition, I was never sure whether I had brought this upon myself or if it was something I had inherited from my father. I knew that while changing one's behavior is possible, becoming someone else is not possible. We are what we are.

My experiences with religion had actually reinforced the message life had already transmitted to me. The only difference was that religion was telling me the consequences of my innate evil would be eternal. I needed someone, or something, to lift me out of this abyss, not push me farther down.

My misunderstanding of two verses in the book of Hebrews (10:26; 12:17) had made me feel God could never forgive me. This coupled with my dream in which my deceased grandmother told me, "God has sent me to tell you that you have stepped into God," had lead me to believe that God had rejected me forever. I thought he was just waiting for nature to take its course so that he could begin my eternal life of misery and pain. I could not convince myself that God really loved me, and I thought that if he couldn't love me, maybe there were others he didn't love too.

The eternal existence and unique position of God had been planted in my mind so firmly there was no way I could deny the reality of it. Not only did I know of his existence, I also knew that he was omnipotent, omniscient, and omnipresent (that is, all-powerful, all-knowing, and present everywhere). I had this drilled into my head so soundly that I couldn't believe there was any place else to turn:

I knew I would never rub the belly of a statue of Buddha in an attempt to get him to belch out an answer to my problems. Nor would I repeat the phrase "There is no god but Allah" until I had convinced him to make me one of his followers. I was absolutely convinced if the God of the Bible had rejected me, there would be no place else to turn. I was also certain if God didn't like me, there must be nothing about me to like.

While I was going through all this internal turmoil, I found a parallel in my spiritual life and my physical life. I had been a foster child in my physical life, and now I was a foster child in my spiritual life. I didn't feel I belonged in any church either.

In an effort to make sense of my situation I read stories of several persons in the Bible that God had chosen as his own: Abraham, Moses, David, Solomon, and many others. I started a list of things God did for these people to see if I could find out how God treated persons he considered to belong to him.

- God protectd Abraham's marriage. He wouldn't even allow his wife wife to be intimate with another person. (Genesis 20)

- He made Abraham wealthy.

- He caused everything Abraham did to prosper. In battle and in life, Abraham was always the winner.

- He saved Moses's life and even allowed Moses's own mother to raise him for some time despite Pharaoh's order that the Hebrew children be killed.

- He made Moses win at everything he did.

- He caused David to be victorious in every battle he fought.

- Even though David committed adultery with Uriah's wife and later caused Uriah to be killed in battle, God said David was a man after his own heart.

- He gave Solomon great wisdom and wealth and caused everything he did to work out well.

It just seemed that all the people God called his own were protected by him from the time they were born until they died. I just couldn't see God's treatment of me as confirmation that I was one of his chosen people.

I heard several "prosperity preachers" state that if God wasn't doing similar things in my life, I just didn't have enough faith, and somehow it was my fault. I also remembered church members saying several things about their personal experiences that just didn't seem to match my own experiences. I just simply didn't fit the Christian mold, and I couldn't figure out what I had done to land in this predicament. I didn't like being a foster child in my earthly home, and I didn't like being a foster child in my religious experience any better.

I read several scriptures in the Bible that were promises I thought God had made to Christians:

- "But they that wait upon the LORD shall renew their strength; they shall mount up with wings as eagles; they shall run, and not be weary; and they shall walk, and not faint." (Isa 40:31)
- " No weapon that is formed against thee shall prosper; and every tongue that shall rise against thee in judgment thou shalt condemn. This is the heritage of the servants of the LORD, and their righteousness is of me, saith the LORD." (Isa 54:17)

A Spiritual Foster Child

- "Ask, and it shall be given you; seek, and ye shall find; knock, and it shall be opened unto you." (Matt 7:7)
- "Teaching them to observe all things whatsoever I have commanded you: and, lo, I am with you always, even unto the end of the world." (Matt 28:20)
- "If ye abide in me, and my words abide in you, ye shall ask what ye will, and it shall be done unto you." (John 15:7)

These verses seemed to indicate that Jesus was involved in every part of life, and no matter what the situation, he was watching, and controlling, everything that happens to every Christian. He was their friend as well as their God.

I couldn't figure out how he could claim to be a friend to me if he just stood by and watched as my father shot my mother at point-blank range with a shotgun and killed her. I was reminded of the elementary school principal who just walked away when I asked him to make the older student stop hurting me. If he had just said one word, "Quit," my hurt would have ended, but instead he said, "There's nothing I can do for you" and walked away.

I wondered if Jesus had said the same thing when my mother was shot and over and over again each time life had dealt me a bad hand. If he is all-powerful and he is really my friend, why didn't he just say, "Quit" or "Don't"?

Why would God allow me to have dreams of my wife cheating on me? Didn't he remember that my dad was so extremely jealous of my mother that he would beat her if he even thought she talked to another man? Didn't he know this brought up feelings of jealousy in me and seemed to confirm that I would "grow up to be just like my father"?. Didn't he know how hard I was trying not to be like my dad? Couldn't he find out that these feelings made me feel ashamed of myself? Why didn't he cause me to have dreams of someone loving me instead of someone disrespecting and rejecting me?

I couldn't help but conclude that these dreams were God's of confirming his rejection of me.

In addition to learning how God treated his chosen people I wanted to learn what actions were required of an individual to become one of his children. Using the following scriptures, I came up with a formula to show what the Bible said about being saved::

- "That if thou shalt confess with thy mouth the Lord Jesus, and shalt believe in thine heart that God hath raised him from the dead, thou shalt be saved." (Rom 10:9)
- "A man that hath friends must shew himself friendly: and there is a friend that sticketh closer than a brother." (Prov 18:24)

- "For God so loved the world that he gave his only begotten Son, that whosoever believeth in him should not perish, but have everlasting life." (John 3:16)
- "And this is the confidence that we have in him, that, if we ask any thing according to his will, he heareth us: And if we know that he hears us, whatsoever we ask, we know that we have the petitions that we desired of him." (1 John 5:14–15)

The formula I developed based on these verses is as follows:

- Confession + belief = salvation
- Salvation = friendship, answered prayers, and eternal life

Working backward, I concluded if God didn't answer my prayers, I had not received his salvation. And if I had not received his salvation, either I had not confessed and believed correctly or I had really been condemned to hell forever without hope. I also concluded that, if the promises that applied to this life didn't apply to me, surely the ones that applied to the afterlife didn't apply to me either.

I made a list of seven requests for God. These requests would match a list of seven promises in the Bible that were made to those who were saved. My requests were:

- Assurance of salvation
- Purpose in life
- Strong desire to accomplish this purpose
- Someone who would be a true friend to encourage me
- Understanding
- Knowledge
- Wisdom

The promises I listed were:

- "Whosoever shall call upon the name of the Lord shall be saved." (Rom 10:13)
- "Ask and you shall receive." (Matt 7:7)
- "Seek and you shall find." (Matt 7:7)
- "Knock and it shall be opened unto you." (Matt 7:7)
- "Call unto me, and I will answer thee, and show thee great and mighty things, which thou knowest not." (Jer 33:3)
- "But thou, when thou prayest, enter into thy closet, and when thou hast shut thy door, pray to thy Father which is in secret; and thy Father which seeth in secret shall reward thee openly." (Matt 6:6)
- "If ye then, being evil, know how to give good gifts unto your children, how much more shall your Father which is

in heaven give good things to them that ask him?" (Matt 7:11)

Now I had seven requests and seven promises that should guarantee God would grant those requests. Using my formula I thought I could find out once and for all just exactly where I stood with God. I wanted to know the truth.

After working on this formula to determine my standing with God, I found that my formula was oversimplified. God does not work like a fast food restaurant: a person can't place an order, pay at the first window, and then pick up the order at the second window.

Studying God's interaction with the biblical personages I discussed previously reveals that God sometimes gives us what we really wanted instead of what we ordered. A good example of this is the account of Abraham's behavior regarding Sodom and Gomorrah. Abraham asked God to spare the two cities. He actually was able to get God to agree that if there were ten righteous persons in the cities, he would not destroy them. God did destroy the cities, but he actually gave Abraham what he really wanted. Abraham wanted God to spare his relatives, and God did exactly that.

God's answers were not always given as quickly as an order from a drive-through at a fast food restaurant. Abraham asked God for a son, but God waited years and years before he finally came through with the answer. When God did answer, he gave Abraham much more than he had requested. In addition to giving Abraham a son, he made him the father of many nations. God also made Abraham the father of his chosen people. God also kept Sarah from beign with another man to assure that Abraham was really the "father of many nations". The bottom line is that God requires us to have a great deal of faith if we are to deal with him.   (By grace are you saved, through faith…Ephesians 2:8)

Fear kept me form doing a lot of reasearch to determine if the troubling verses in Hebrews had a different meaning. I knew that sometimes it can take a multitude of positive statements to overcome a single negative one I also knew, if I ever made it out of this hole, the climb was certainly going to be steep.

I finally realized that knowing for certain that God had rejected me forever couldn't be any worse than living as though he had. It was time to face this problem once and for all.

I knew it was time for me to find the truth and face reality. If the truth turned out to be that God had rejected me forever, I would do my best to enjoy as much of the time I had left in this life as I could. If God had not rejected me, I would be able to rid myself of the doubts and fears that were causing my life to be something less than enjoyable.

A Spiritual Foster Child

Previous experience had taught me that I would not be able to depend on the teachings or practices of others. I knew that no pastor would be tell me even if he believed I was headed for hell with no possibility of redemption. I wanted to know the truth. This path could only be traveled in "single-file". I knew I would be on my own, and I was not at all sure I was ready to accept what I was about to learn, but better now than later, I thought.

I decided to shut out all outside influences and read the Bible again and again until the answers became crystal-clear. I had faced my other problems, and so I would face this one too.

I was determined to find the truth and accept my fate. I might not be able to make sweet lemonade from the basket of lemons life had given me, but I knew I could at least accept the truth and put the problem behind me—or, in this case, postpone my punishment until it was due, that is, after my death.

Am I My Father's Son?

Putting the Pieces Together

When a builder begins to construct a house, the first step in the process is to create an architectural drawing with a detailed construction plan and a list of materials needed to finish the project. I decided that building my spiritual life would require a similar approach.

If the plan were to rocket me out of my state of confusion it would need to provide answers to several very difficult questions.

The first question, of course, was: How does a person become a follower of Christ—is it necessary to go before the congregation and kneel down at a bench in front of a church?

The second question was: Is a person required to beg God for salvation, and if so, how long does it take, and how intense does the begging need to be?

The third question was: How could God claim to be my friend and allow bad things to happen to me? I believed he was watching when my mother was shot, and I believed he knew about my struggles with religion and all the other problems I had faced. I didn't see that his actions were the kind of actions one would expect from a friend.

The fourth question was: If a person is saved and then is disobedient to God, is that person without hope, as Hebrews 10:26 seems to indicate?

The fifth question was: What is the sin that God will not forgive?

And finally, the sixth question was: How does a person know God has in fact saved him or her, and how will that person know for sure he or she hasn't missed a step and won't wind up on the wrong side of God at the judgment (as in the sheep on God's right and the goats on his left (Matt 25:32–33)?

There are numerous stories in the Bible that give examples of persons being saved. I used these to help me find answers to my first question. One of the best ones is found in Acts 8:34–39:

> And the eunuch answered Philip, and said, I pray thee, of whom speaketh the prophet this? Of himself, or of some other man?
>
> Then Philip opened his mouth, and began at the same scripture, and preached unto him Jesus.
>
> And as they went on their way, they came unto a certain water: and the eunuch said, See, here is water; what doth hinder me to be baptized?

> And Philip said, If thou believest with all thine heart, thou mayest. And he answered and said, I believe that Jesus Christ is the Son of God.
>
> And he commanded the chariot to stand still: and they went down both into the water, both Philip and the eunuch; and he baptized him.
>
> And when they were come up out of the water, the Spirit of the Lord caught away Philip, that the eunuch saw him no more: and he went on his way rejoicing.

There was not an altar in this salvation experience. There wasn't even a church building. Actually, the person who was saved was sitting on a wagon seat(a chariot). Also, there was no begging and no crying. The eunuch simply said, "I believe. Why can't I be baptized?" And Peter said, "If you believe, you may."

Revelations 3:20 also confirms that it is not necessary to beg God for salvation: "Behold, I stand at the door, and knock: if any man hears my voice, and opens the door, I will come in to him, and will eat with him, and he with me."

Jesus Christ extends the invitation. Those who accept his invitation are saved. It is similar to receiving a wedding invitation that requires an RSVP: the recipient simply must respond that he or she will be there and then must show up on time. And, by the way, the invitation for salvation has been extended to everyone.

Romans 10:13 says, "Whosoever shall call upon the name of the Lord shall be saved." Or, to use my analogy again, accept the invitation, RSVP, and then show up.

Acts 16:30–34 is another excellent example of how to be saved:

> [The jailor] brought them [Paul and Silas] out, and said, Sirs, what must I do to be saved?
> And they said, Believe on the Lord Jesus Christ, and thou shalt be saved, and thy house.
> And they spake unto him the word of the Lord, and to all that were in his house.
> And he took them the same hour of the night, and washed their stripes; and was baptized, he and all his, straightway.
> And when he had brought them into his house, he set meat before them, and rejoiced, believing in God with all his house.

Therefore, the answer to question number one is that a person is saved if he or she believes that Jesus Christ is the Son of God and that all authority has been given to him, including the ability to forgive sins. After believing this, the person makes a public confession of what he or she has believed.

The answer to my second question is that no begging is required to be saved. Jesus comes looking for us, not the other way around. "For the son of man is come to seek and to save that which was lost." (Luke 19:10)

I found the best answer to my third question (How could Jesus claim to be my friend and seemingly offer no help when I needed it badly?) in the book of Hebrews: "Although he was a Son, he learned obedience from the things which he suffered." (Heb 5:8). This verse refers to Jesus and the things he suffered on the cross and in every aspect of his life.

This verse taught me that there is a new covenant between God and man or a different way of accomplishing God's purpose in the life of his chosen people. Under the old covenant God blessed Israel to show the world the benefit of serving him, but Jesus suffered the curse of the cross. Jesus said his followers would suffer in the same way he had suffered. (John 15:20) If God watched his Son die and his son learned obedience from this experience, maybe he allows us to have a few problems and learn a thing or two from them.

The third question was also answered by a personal experience. I actually stopped asking God this question. Instead, I asked the following question: "Will you please show me how you love me even in the problems I have experienced?" I confessed to him that his word was true and that I knew I must be wrong in my assumption that he didn't love me.

A few weeks after I prayed this prayer, I saw one of my mother's cousins at the graveyard during a Saturday clean-up. He was talking to some friends of mine about life in the 40'' and 50's.

I asked him if he remembered what had happened the day my mother was shot. He said, "Yes, but your aunt, Ruth, was there and she could tell you much more about it." I made a mental note that I would try to locate her and talk with her about it.

'The next Saturday I was back at the cemetery to place flowers on my mother's grave. While I was doing this, my wife looked down at the grave and found a set of keys. The keys had an "Ace Rewards" tag attached to them with a member number and a toll free number to call.

I called the number and the person that answered the phone said she could not give out member information but she would call the member.

She placed me on hold while she made the call. She came back on the line and told me the person did not have transportation to come get the keys but she agreed to allow me to have her phone number.

Putting The Pieces Together

I called the number and, just as soon as the phone was answered, I knew it was my aunt Ruth. (the person my mother's cousin had told me about the week before)

When I took the keys to her house and gave them to her, I asked if I could talk with her for a few minutes. She agreed and we talked for a while about what had happened rthe day my mother was shot.

Then, just out of the blue, she said, "Your mother was not saved when your dad shot her. She lived for about thirty minutes and a lady came in that knew the Bible and led your mother to Christ." In other words, God gave my mother thirty minutes in order to be saved and now he is keeping her in heaven for me until we are reunited again.

I now knew how God could say he loved me when he let those things happen to me.

That might well have been the only circumstance in which my mother would have been saved. I felt both joy and shame. I was joyful that God had given mom enough time to change her eternal destiny before she died, but I felt ashamed that I had questioned his love for me.

Not all of God's people have identical experiences. Each of us are called to accomplish a different objective, and we have different life experiences to accomplish his purpose in our lives.

This was true under the old covenant, and it is also true under the new covenant.

I fould several answers to my questions about marriage difficulties. Not every relationship with God comes with the same "protection clauses." God provided a "marriage protection" plan to Abraham and Isaac. (He would not allow Sarah or Rebekah to become intimately involved with other men.)(Genesis 12:10-20, Genesis 20, and Genesis 26)

Hosea's marriage was not protected by God. A quick read of the book of Hosea reveals that God required Hosea to marry a prostitute, and when she went back to her former trade, Hosea bought her freedom again and forgave her unfaithfulness. By the names God commanded Hosea to give his children, there is strong evidence Hosea's wife was unfaithful to him even when they were together. (God told Hosea to name one son a Hebrew name meaning "you are not my son.")

God wanted Hosea to endure the humiliation of an unfaithful spouse in order for him to better understand the hurt God feels when his people are unfaithful to him. It is easy to imagine that Hosea always thought any man he met on the street might have had a relationship with his wife. He may even have been talking to someone about the latter's spiritual welfare and at the same time may have thought, "I wonder if this man is the father of my child." This is a terrible humiliation, but one that God allowed him to endure.

Maybe God gave me the dreams to let me have a better understanding of how Jesus feels about His Church being involved in so many other things besides preaching the gospel.

The examples of Jesus's crucifixion and of Hosea led me to realize that God is more interested in our eternal future than in our temporary comfort. If we are his, he will provide us with everything we need to accomplish His, not our, purpose, and sometimes what we need includes an assortment of very difficult problems.

I also learned that God uses things that may be hurtful to us to help us understand how he feels when we are unfaithful to him. My lack of faith in him must have cut him very deeply, especially after all he had done for me. Maybe my dreams were his way of letting me know I was hurting him by my lack of faith.

I struggled with answering my fourth question much more than with my previous questions. (Is it true that after being saved, if a person disobeys God, that person is lost forever because of this act of disobedience?) Finding the answer was more difficult for me because I was not sure I really wanted to know the answer. As long as the slightest doubt remained, I would not be forced to accept my future role in the eternal flames of hell. I was horribly afraid that the answer would be the one I did not want to face: that God will not forgive someone who sins after being saved.

I finally decided I would have to find out either sooner or later, and sooner would be better than later. Maybe there might be an escape from the eternal destiny I had assumed to be mine.

I knew that finding answers to this question would require me to know more about God's dealings with mankind: all the way from Adam to Moses, from Moses to Jesus, and from Jesus until now.

I was forced to read the Bible and interpret it for myself. I shut out all TV preachers and other persons who professed to speak on God's behalf. I wanted to know for myself what the Bible said about God's judgments regarding mankind's sins. I did occasionally listen to one Bible teacher on TV who covered topics that interested me.

I found three approaches God used to deal with mankind and sin. The first one was his treatment of the actions of those who lived from Adam to Moses. The Bible says God did not count sin against humans before he gave the law to Moses and the Hebrews. "For until the law sin was in the world: but sin is not imputed when there is no law" (Rom 5:13).

Putting The Pieces Together

Abraham married his half-sister, which was forbidden in the law God gave to Moses. Even though Abraham did this, it was not counted against him. Also, one of Jacob's sons had an affair with one of Jacob's concubines. This too would have been forbidden by the law God later gave to the Hebrews. There are also several other actions of the patriarchs listed in the Bible that would have been against the Mosaic law, but none of these actions were counted against those who committed them. One such example is that Abraham's nephew, Lot, got drunk and had sex with his daughters. He actually had children by both his daughters. (Gen 19)

God's second approach was to require man to live by the law. During this period God actually did count sin against people. Disobeying the law was sin, and this disobedience required various levels of punishment.

After Moses received the law, the Israelites were actually commanded to execute a man for picking up sticks on the Sabbath day. God had now started keeping track of sins and punishing his people when they failed to be obedient:

> And while the children of Israel were in the wilderness, they found a man that gathered sticks upon the Sabbath day.
> And they that found him gathering sticks brought him unto Moses and Aaron, and unto all the congregation.

And they put him in ward, because it was not declared what should be done to him.

And the LORD said unto Moses, The man shall be surely put to death: all the congregation shall stone him with stones without the camp.

And all the congregation brought him without the camp, and stoned him with stones, and he died; as the LORD commanded Moses. (Num 15:32–36)

What was God trying to accomplish with the law? In Galatians 3 the Bible gives a reason for the law and its harshness: "Wherefore the law was our schoolmaster to bring us unto Christ, that we might be justified by faith" (Gal 3:24). The law was given to demonstrate to mankind that being righteous was not something any individual could accomplish. In other words, the law could only lead to one thing, the sacrifice of Jesus on the cross.

The third approach was grace. It is somewhat similar to the first approach. The difference is that if a person's sin is not to be imputed to him or her, it must be imputed to Jesus Christ instead. Yes, we have sinned, as Isaiah said: "All we like sheep have gone astray; we have turned every one to his own way; and the LORD hath laid on him the iniquity of us all" (Isa 53:6). Romans 3:23 also says that we have all sinned, but Romans 6:23 says, "The gift of God is eternal life." In other words, the sins of those who are saved are added to Jesus Christ's account, not to their own accounts.

Now, why does the book of Hebrews say that if we sin willfully we have no other sacrifice for sin? The practice of trying to be righteous in order to be saved only leads to one thing: failure. The end of the law was the sacrifice of Jesus Christ for sins. If we were to return to attempting to keep the law in order to be saved, this would lead to the same place, his crucifixion, and he is not going there again.

If we choose the law as our road to heaven, we will be disappointed, because this path doesn't lead to heaven. Christ's crucifixion washed out and made impassable the road of the old law, and now the animal sacrifices are no longer effective. Therefore, we no longer make sacrificial offerings for sin because no more sacrifices are needed: "Neither by the blood of goats and calves, but by his own blood he entered in once into the holy place, having obtained eternal redemption *for us*" (Heb 9:12); "For by grace are ye saved through faith; and that not of yourselves: it is the gift of God: Not of works, lest any man should boast" (Eph 2:8–9).

Up to this point, as I mentioned previously, my self-esteem tank was running way below empty. I was trying to be as good as I thought everyone else was. I was also trying to be good enough so that God would have no choice but to save me. In other words, I was going in the opposite direction of salvation. I was trying to keep the law, but the law only led to Christ's crucifixion.

What God wanted from me was not to appear before him clothed in my own righteousness. Instead, he wanted me to recognize that, no matter how hard I tried, I couldn't keep the law. Even if I were able to keep it perfectly in the future, I had broken the law in the past, and that required payment. As a matter of fact, I didn't even know all the law, which is set forth in Exodus, Leviticus, Numbers, and Deuteronomy. (If anyone thinks he or she has lived a perfect life, I suggest that that person spend time reading these books.) I realized God was not trying to punish me for my sins; rather, he was trying to save me from my sins by drawing my attention to the fact that I was on the wrong road.

Another tough question for me was my fifth question: What is the sin that God will not forgive? The only answer I found was that God will not forgive us if we fail to accept his plan of salvation. In Romans 10:9–13 the scripture plainly states that all who believe in and confess Christ will be saved. Based on this statement, it follows that those who do not believe and do not confess will not be saved. This is the only reference I could find to persons not making it to heaven.

Also, in Revelations the Bible says that all individuals who have their names written in the Book of Life are welcomed into heaven. According to the Bible the only way to get one's name written in the Book of Life is to accept God's plan of salvation. (Luke 10:20)

My last question—"How does someone know that he or she is saved?"—is the most important question and is very difficult for me to answer. I will deal with it later in this book.

Am I My Father's Son?

Weighing the Evidence

When I made the decision to find the truth one of the first things I learned is that not all "preachers" have a biblical basis for what they are selling to the public. Some of these self-appointed teachers seem to be more interested in making money than they are in preaching the truth.

I had always been taught to respect anyone calling themselves a "Christian" or a "preacher," but these materialistic preachers made it impossible for me to respect them. I just couldn't swallow the medicine they were prescribing. I felt the side effects would cause more problems than their cures would prevent.

Mathew 28:19 clearly states the mission of the church. ("Go ye therefore, and teach all nations, baptizing them in the name of the Father, and of the Son, and of the Holy Ghost:") In spite if this directive more and more so-called Christian theologians seemed to be spending their time promoting their own theories rather than telling the world about the true nature of God and his plan of salvation.

A good example of this detour from God's directive is the amount of energy wasted on the creation story. Contrary to the proclamations of a number of so-called theologians, the book of Genesis was not written so Christians could argue with scientists about the age of the earth. Rather, it was written so the Israelites would understand God's ownership of his creation. The first verse of the Bible, Genesis 1:1, says that God created the heavens and the earth. Chapter 1 continues to say that not only did God create the heavens and the earth, he created everything that exists. In John 1:1–14 the Bible actually says Jesus created everything:

> In the beginning was the Word, and the Word was with God, and the Word was God.
>
> The same was in the beginning with God.
>
> All things were made by him; and without him was not any thing made that was made.
>
> In him was life; and the life was the light of men.
>
> And the light shineth in darkness; and the darkness comprehended it not.
>
> There was a man sent from God, whose name was John.
>
> The same came for a witness, to bear witness of the Light that all men through him might believe.
>
> He was not that Light, but was sent to bear witness of that Light.
>
> That was the true Light, which lighteth every man that cometh into the world.
>
> He was in the world, and the world was made by him, and the world knew him not.

> He came unto his own, and his own received him not.
>
> But as many as received him, to them gave he power to become the sons of God, even to them that believe on his name:
>
> Which were born, not of blood, nor of the will of the flesh, nor of the will of man, but of God.
>
> And the Word was made flesh, and dwelt among us, (and we beheld his glory, the glory as of the only begotten of the Father,) full of grace and truth.

Regardless of one's opinion about how God created mankind, according to the Bible, he is responsible for our existence.

If God created everything, it follows that everything he created belongs to him and he has the right to do with it what he will. Also, if he created it and he is a loving God, he would want it to survive and do well. His purpose is to preserve—not to destroy—mankind and all his creation.

The Genesis story says that God formed man out of the dust of the ground. When he created humans, he gave them the ability to produce offspring. According to the Bible, every human owes his or her existence to mankind's ability to procreate. Since God created the process that would later produce my body, he has clear title to all I am or will ever be. There is no question in my mind about ownership: God is ultimately responsible for my existence, and therefore God is the father of my natural body.

Genesis also records the account of mankind's disobedience to God. Mankind became aligned with Satan instead of God when Adam and Eve rejected God's plan for life and chose to follow Satan's leadership. In other words, we chose to be the property of another god. Since our allegiance is now to Satan rather than to God, we have become spiritually separated from God. The question then becomes: Is God my spiritual father?

According to the book of Genesis God chose the Israelites to be His own. He later made his first covenant with them. Under this covenant, obedience produced blessings, and disobedience caused God's wrath to come upon them.

Because I am a Gentile and this covenant only included the Israelites, it is likely my ancestors were not included. I can find no information in the Bible to clarify our standing while the Israelites were subject to the law.

However, according to the New Testament, when Jesus was crucified God established a new covenant that includes all peoples of the earth (Rom 7:1–6):

> Know ye not, brethren, (for I speak to them that know the law,) how that the law hath dominion over a man as long as he liveth?
>
> For the woman which hath an husband is bound by the law to her husband so long as he liveth; but if the husband be dead, she is loosed from the law of her husband.
>
> So then if, while her husband liveth, she be married to another man, she shall be called an adulteress: but if her husband be dead, she is free from that law; so that she is no adulteress, though she be married to another man.
>
> Wherefore, my brethren, ye also are become dead to the law by the body of Christ; that ye should be married to another, even to him who is raised from the dead, that we should bring forth fruit unto God.
>
> For when we were in the flesh, the motions of sins, which were by the law, did work in our members to bring forth fruit unto death.
>
> But now we are delivered from the law, that being dead wherein we were held; that we should serve in newness of spirit, and not in the oldness of the letter.

The writer of the book of Romans is using the marriage between a man and woman to symbolize mankind's obligation to the law as opposed to the covenant of grace. Basically, he is saying the law no longer exists as an agreement between God and man. It is dead, and therefore, mankind is free to accept the new covenant. While the law was based on the actions of mankind (mankind's obedience or disobedience to the law), the new covenant is *not* based on mankind's continued obedience. It is based entirely on the grace of God, and our only requirement is to accept God's blessings as a free gift: This is grace, or unmerited favor.

In our human system of laws, a legal contract is binding if a person makes an offer, another accepts the offer, and consideration is exchanged between the two parties. God's new covenant is a contract between him and mankind and I believe God abides by these same binding rules.

For example, if I were to publish an offer in the newspaper stating that I would give one hundred dollars to anyone who walked across the George Washington Bridge before noon on June 14, 2023, I would be obligated by law to pay one hundred dollars to anyone who did what I asked.

My offer would be available to anyone that walked across the bridge during the specified time. The second party's acceptance of my offer would be his or her act of walking across the bridge during the specified time. The consideration would be the one hundred dollars that I would give and the walk that the other party would perform.

Weighing the Evidence

I would receive the satisfaction of knowing that the person had walked across the bridge, and he or she would receive the one hundred dollars. If I published such an offer and you walked across the bridge during the specified time but were unable to collect the money from me, you could sue me for the hundred dollars, and no judge would refuse to rule in your favor.

God has published an even better offer: "If thou shall confess with thy mouth the Lord Jesus and believe in thine heart that God has raised him from the dead, thou shalt be saved" (Rom 10:9).

An individual accepts this offer by performing the actions God requests: believe and confess. The consideration God gives to mankind is salvation; the consideration mankind gives to God is recognition of His Son as the risen Lord and Savior. It is a binding contract, and, if a person believes and confesses, God is obligated to pay what he promised: salvation. He has no choice but to keep his agreement. ("In hope of eternal life, which God, that cannot lie, promised before the world began;") (Titus 1:2)

Whether the value of the consideration given is equal to the value of that received is not an issue. On the surface, it would seem that what God gives to mankind is of much higher value than what mankind gives to God in exchange. Eternal life (and all that goes with salvation) seems to be of much higher value than believing that Jesus is the Son of God and that God raised Him from the dead, but there may be some things we do not know.

John 3:16 says that God loved the world enough to give His Son for our salvation.

Maybe God loves his Son enough to make him "Lord of Lords" and "King of Kings," and our recognition of him as such helps to accomplish this purpose. Regardless of the equality of consideration, or lack thereof, God is the author of the covenant/contract, and he decided what price we would pay. He also decided what he would give in exchange for our payment.

So how do we know we are saved? The Bible says, "The Spirit itself beareth witness with our spirit, that we are the children of God" (Rom 8:16), It also says, "We know that we have passed from death unto life, because we love the brethren. He that loveth not *his* brother abideth in death" (1 John 3:14).

As parents we deal with each of our children differently. The needs of one child may be different than the needs of another child. Therefore, our treatment of each is personalized. In other words, we do not do exactly the same thing for every one of our children. Rather, we attempt to reach them where they are.

God deals with us in a similar fashion. Why did God allow me to be confused about whether he really loved me? Actually, his treatment of me was not that different from his treatment of the Hebrew slaves when he brought them into the wilderness.

Weighing the Evidence

He gave them water and food, but first he let them get really thirsty and really hungry.

Why didn't he give each of them a fanny pack with a replicator. like the one from *Star Trek* that would create food on demand. It would dispense a variety of food and drink? Then the Israelites would have been able to select something for breakfast, something else for lunch, and then an entirely different meal for dinner. If God was able to make the loaves and fishes feed five thousand, surely he would have been able to come up with a compact vending machine that manufactured any food item on the fly.

He treated the Israelites the way he did so they would experience hunger. By experiencing hunger and thirst, they would gain a much better understanding of the needs these items fulfill in the natural body.

Similarly, I would never have studied the Bible for myself had I not known the awful feelings of loneliness and rejection. Neither would I have attempted to write this book, which I sincerely hope will benefit others who may be going through similar experiences.

Even though I thought God had rejected me forever, he only wanted to teach me just how valuable and important his salvation is to mankind. He wanted me to have no other place to go but to him. My requests that he fill the void left by my mother's death, that he salvage my rocky marriage, and that he meet my other needs went unanswered simply because I had a much greater need that he wanted to fill. I needed God. He allowed everything to be taken away so I would have no choice but to turn to him.

He gave me dreams to help me learn how to solve my problems. Also, I think he wanted me to know how he feels when his church becomes interested in other things and leaves his mission unfinished. He did this by allowing me to have dreams of my wife cheating on me. His church is cheating on him and he wanted me to have an idea of the heartache this is causing him.

It was not until I started writing this book that I realized part of this truth. I know God answered my prayer when I asked him if I could be saved and he caused the preacher to preach on healing. After I attended an Arkansas Baptist Convention where Dr. W. A. Criswell preached a sermon in which he said that "stepped into God" means "became dear to God," I came to understand why God gave me the dream in which my grandmother told me that he had sent her to say to me that I had stepped into God. I now know this meant that the message God was sending me was not that he had rejected me but that I had "become dear" to him. I later learned Dr. Criswell used this phrase to refer to someone who had been saved. God did not single me out and make me more important than anyone else. He just had to reach farther down to get to me.

Weighing the Evidence

The bottom line is God loved me enough to allow me to learn all these lessons even though I was whining about my troubles all along the way. He didn't give up on me, and I know if God can love me, he can love anyone—especially you.

Lessons Learned

Some of the most important things I have learned are:

1. No matter how alone we feel, there is always someone who cares.

2. I am not the only one who has faced problems like mine.

3. I am a better person because I decided to control my problems instead of allowing my problems to control me.

4. If I cannot solve my problems, I can grow strong enough to live with them.

5. Only those who have fought life's battles can stand in the victor's circle.

6. Those that cower under the banner of self-pity and defeat can never experience the exhilaration that comes only from being a winner.

7. Every individual is a potential winner and/or a potential loser. Each of us is standing, or will stand, at a crossroads in our lives where we are the only one who can make the decision to win or lose.

8. It is never too late to decide to control our own destiny.

9. And finally, perhaps the most important thing I have learned is that we are the only ones who can give our problems permission to pin our shoulders to the ground and declare victory over us.

My life is not perfect, but it is much better than it could have been. My children never called anyone else "Daddy". They both accepted Christ as their savior because I took them to church. My son is now in heaven because of this.

Although my marriage is not what either of us, my wife and I, would have liked for it to be, it has lasted fifty-seven years. Would it have been possible for both of us to have had better relationships? Yes! But unfortunately trying to find a better life would have come at a high cost to others, so I believe making the most of it was the correct decision.

It is easy to write a single paragraph that covers one's activity for a period of several years. But sometimes such succinctness oversimplifies problems and their resolutions. The truth is that answers to some of my questions came very slowly. As a matter of fact, I wrestled with the question of whether I had lost my salvation for several years before I found a completely satisfactory answer.

Have I arrived at a place in life where no problems exist? Do I know everything about God and his plans for mankind—past, present, and future?

Lessons Learned

The obvious answer to all these questions is a resounding *"no."*

The Bible says that "life is short and full of trouble" (Job 14:1). A vocational school instructor of mine summed up my findings as well as anyone could. She said, "I am not going to teach you everything you need to know. I am going to teach you where to look when you need answers to your questions."

Learning to use this approach to life's problems produces much better results than attempting to solve all existing problems before moving to the next level.

If all we do is solve the problems we have today, we fall short of acquiring the ability to make life more enjoyable. As long as we are alive, we will encounter new problems, and these problems will always need to be solved.

My experience has taught me to look for three kinds of problems: (1) problems I can solve by myself, (2) problems that have no solution, and (3) problems that can only be solved with help from others.

When I finally recognized that my feeling of low self-esteem could be corrected by my own efforts, I was able to reduce this feeling to a manageable level.

I have learned that problems are not meant to defeat us. If they are handled correctly, they will actually make us stronger.

God did not remove all the Israelites' enemies from the land of Canaan because he wanted his people to be reminded of their inability to exist without him. Likewise, I think we all need an occasional problem to remind us we cannot exist in our own sphere, independent of God and friends.

Another problem actually moved into the category of those I could solve with my own effort. It was my problem with religion. God brought me to a place that required my own strength to move forward. Then he left the rest up to me.

There is a religious joke that goes something like this:

There was a flood raging in a small village. Officials were using boats to rescue citizens of the small town, and they came to a gentleman and asked him to get in the boat. He told them God was going to rescue him, so they left him alone. The water continued to rise, so another boat came around, and they also asked him to get in the boat. He told them God would take care of him. Soon the water had almost covered the entire house, and the gentleman climbed up on the top of the roof. A helicopter came by and asked him to get in. He told the pilot God would take care of him. Finally, the man drowned. When he got to heaven, he asked God why he didn't rescue him. God told him, "I sent you two boats and a helicopter. What more did you want?"

God allowed me to have the dream about the bicycle I was struggling to drag behind me instead of riding. This taught me my problems were really my vehicle to ride toward a successful life. He sent a boat.

By causing the preacher to preach on healing, God confirmed that I was someone who was eligible for salvation. He sent another boat. I just needed to climb in.

He gave me the dream in which my grandmother gave me the message. He then sent the pastor of the First Baptist Church of Dallas, Texas, to tell me what the words meant. He sent the helicopter.

My reliance on what others said about their religious experience was taking me in the wrong direction. It was not until I decided I needed to take the initiative and find answers myself that this problem began to be solved: I just needed to climb aboard the vehicle God sent to me.

As for the second category, that of problems that cannot be solved, I realized that my inability to bring my mother back to life was one such problem. This was a problem that could not be solved. No matter how much I wanted her to be with me, it was not going to happen. Nor was anyone going to replace her. I was never going to have a mother no matter how hard I tried. I needed to accept this cold hard fact and move on.

I wanted to have my own "father" to take me fishing and help me make it through the difficult times in life. It was not going to happen.

No matter how much time I spent feeling sorry for myself, these facts were not going to change. Dwelling on what I didn't have was wasting a great deal of my time. I needed to throw these problems over my shoulders and try to manipulate my attitude toward them until my mind no longer focused entirely on them. I called this putting them behind me in my "backpack". They were still there but they became easier to handle. I was controlling their impact on my life instead of letting them rule over me.

If I had put these two problems and other unsolvable problems in my backpack earlier and carried them, I could have moved through life with much greater ease. When I stopped looking for a mother and a father, it became easier for me to concentrate my efforts on solving other problems that actually had a solution. The past can never be changed. Sometimes we just need to readjust our backpack of problems and plow through life until we gain the strength necessary to carry these problems.

When my son died in November 2007, a gentleman who attended the funeral, and who had lost his own son a few years earlier, gave me a word of encouragement. He said, "Joe, you are never going to get over this. You will eventually be able to deal with it, but the hurt will never stop." He was absolutely correct in his prediction. I had to put this in my backpack too.

Occasionally, when things are quiet and I am alone, this hurt raises its head, and I find my heart aching for my son as tears well up in my eyes. But the hurt eventually subsides without consuming my entire life.

I miss my son, and I always will, but I realize that I must live for him instead of with him. He will never come back to me, so I will wait to be reunited with him when I go where he is.

And finally, as for the third category of problems, we all need friends to help us through some of life's difficult times. I would never have been able to dig myself out of the pit I found myself in when I decided to drop out of high school. My friends kept me from making a mistake that would have resulted in an entirely different life for me.

I would not have been able to pay college tuition if the man I had hated for many years had not left me enough money for me to pay the expenses. Even though he had not been much of a father to me, he did provide the money I needed to get my business administration degree from Southwest Baptist University.

The bottom line is that whether we can solve our problems alone, with help, or not at all, no problem is too difficult to keep us from our destiny. My sincere hope is that you the reader find the way to beat any problems you have. Who knows—someday you may be the person who makes a difference in the lives of my grandchildren or great-grandchildren.

My prayer for you is that God will do through you everything he is big enough and powerful enough to do.

www.ingramcontent.com/pod-product-compliance
Lightning Source LLC
Chambersburg PA
CBHW071303040426
42444CB00009B/1853